Tr

- When Life Changes

Author:
Doug Booker
www.bookertraining.com

Contributing Writer:
Christopher Kirby, MD

Publisher:
Drambert Publishing Company

'Triangles, Compasses & GOD'
2013 © Doug Booker.
(Revision, Jan 2015)

ISBN-13: 978-1506018843
ISBN-10: 150601884X

(Also available on Kindle)

Printed in the USA

Table of Contents

Dedication

Without a doubt, I am dedicating this to my Mom and Dad as the ones who steered my path, acted as my compass and who held key spots in my triangle.

Both of my parents, who I loved dearly and I owe much, passed away in 2013 leaving a significant void in my life.

My earthly father and 'dad' left us just this month, Dec 2013; Mom this past January. With the grief of losing two most dearly beloved friends from my life, the Good Lord provides me plenty of peace. This 'peace' is about which I wrote this book.

Thanks Mother and Father for all you were to me and for me; because you loved me and I loved you.

Thank You God for them.

Foreword

(By my good friend Chris Kirby, MD)

"The Lord God said, "It is not good for the man to be alone..." Genesis 2:18

The compass, first invented by the Chinese over 2000 years ago, is a navigational tool used to help the user to know what direction they are traveling. When they chart their course of travel it must be determined which direction relative to the four quadrants (N, S, E, and W) one must travel to arrive at their destination. The compass points to north so travel can be guided relative to that north point. The compass points to magnetic north vs. true north so correction must be calculated by the traveler. There are variables that can cause the compass to deviate from magnetic north. If the user is unaware of these factors and do not make corrections they can start the journey in the correct direction but end up miles from their destination. In life and in relationships we need a "Life" compass that is infallible and points to truth or we too can start in the right direction and find ourselves far from our goal or destination. A relational compass is essential for the health and growth of a healthy bonding between people.

Life is all about relationships. Everything- yes everything- we do on a daily basis is relational. We can argue that when alone we are not involved in anything relational. The truth is that even when alone we are still being relational in that the relationship is us with-ourselves. In every relationship there are different levels of intimacy-

IN –TO- ME- SEE

 Intimacy refers to the level or degree in which we allow others to see our true self. My most intimate relationship is with God and with myself. The degree of intimacy shared with others is based on degrees of trust and shared willingness to be open and honest. Since God knew me before I existed and He is forever trustworthy and true the relational intimacy is only limited by my willingness to be totally honest, vulnerable, and trusting of Him. He knows my innermost thoughts and feeling yet I must be willing to express them to Him as best I can.

All relationships are a direct line connection either close or distant based on the level of intimacy. This is measured not in physical separation but in a spiritual connection. My closes friend, Tito, lives over 1000 miles away yet we are connected in the spiritual sense as if we were side by side. I can be standing next to a person unknown by me in a crowd yet have a relationship that is only connected by the fact that we are two people experiencing similar locality and whatever the reason for us to be in that crowded situation.

In all relationships there is a balance. The connection is affected by the degree in which we are willing to share intimacy. Are we selfish, self centered, self serving, less than trustworthy and honest or are we selfless, other focused, sacrificial, open and honest? We can deceive ourselves in believing we are always the latter but in reality the former is always part of our innermost humanness. As a physician my relationships with my patients were serving and other focused but not truly sacrificial in that I was compensated for my services. The fulcrum on which that relational straight line connection rests is what is known as the "human condition". Since we as being human are imperfect the likelihood is that that relational line will frequently if not always be unbalanced unless we turn to a "power greater than ourselves" as the source of relational balance.

I have come to know, trust, and rely upon Jesus as my one and only true source of relational balance and for my ability to know/- true intimacy with others. Instead of my relationships being perched on my self-will I have learned to look upward (actually inward for Christ through the Holy Spirit dwells within me) and attempt to have all relationships to be three way-myself, others, and with Jesus Christ as the cornerstone. The connection goes from a relationship between two people perched on an unsteady fulcrum to one that is a triangle in which Jesus is at the apex forever supporting us.

What determines whether the triangle is an isosceles (two equal sides) with the equal sides pointed towards Jesus versus a scalene (unequal sides) is based on each person's willingness to turn to Jesus as the source of all power and relational balance. This book outlines why this is essential and describes a journey towards that self discovery.

Christopher Kirby MD

"And what does the LORD require of you? To act justly & to love mercy & to walk humbly with your God."
Micah 6:8

❖ Chris Kirby was a High School classmate of mine who now 40 years later I have crossed paths with again. I am sure he has been led into my life and I am thankful for his friendship in my world again!

Purpose / Introduction

"For everything there is a season, and a time for every matter under heaven..."
Ecclesiastes 3:1

First and foremost, as the scripture above goes, it is my season to share this – it is time.

It is CHRISTmas 2013 as I am wrapping up this book. It is a tough one with both parents passing away this year; this will be my first CHRISTmas without my 'Mommy and Daddy'. I had them for 58 years of my life, which makes me pretty fortunate in comparison to many. It is on my heart on so many levels. My loss of them has much to do with the reason and purpose for this book being written at this time. As I struggle in pursuing the usual laughter and enjoyment of the Season, it makes me realize I am being caught up and overwhelmed with my human relationships. Instead of the ONE I should be focusing on...

To begin specifically focusing us, this book is about an amazing realization arrived at over the course of a few critical years. This was after years of well... turbulent times in my 'unrealized' mode.

Right now you might be thinking, 'what did he say?' Stick with me.

This purpose & introduction along with the first chapter will take some concentration on your part. Find a quiet moment and place; then digest what this is all about my friend.

This writing is primarily about YOU; but also about all of us humans – the people of this world of ours. My intent here is to share a dynamic uncovered along my journey; a very specific and central aspect of life leading to who I 'am' now. This is all about a reality that changed my life in extremely GOOD ways. I totally hope you will internalize the message here and come to the peace of mind that I have about this 'realization'.

Let me be clear here. This is about my faith, story and beliefs. However this is NOT about me preaching at you or trying to cause you to buy into my beliefs. Well, sort of I guess it is (GRIN). It is about my God, Jesus Christ and the deity in which I do indeed believe.

My God is the God, which is what I believe. I appreciate others have other gods; this message is for you as well I believe. Let me put it this way: for any learning, personal change or take-away to occur here, it is critical that you are someone who accepts there is 'something or someone bigger' than YOU and I and the rest of us humans of this planet.

Q: Is there a higher authority of some kind that leads your spiritual being that you subscribe to, pray to and seek when you realize you are not enough on your own?

That is WHO (and what) this is about, YOU and your god. Again to repeat, for me, that higher-authority is the One God, Jesus Christ and the Holy Spirit.

NOTE: *I am kind of assuming something here in these regards. If you have a god other than mine, if 'he, she or it' is real - then all this applies I would think?!? This is all about whomever or whatever god may be yours. For me, that's*

again the GOD of the bible, Jesus Christ and the Holy Spirit
– the three I believe are ONE.

Yours? That's for you to work through I reckon' ☺*.*

Is your god one that fits into your life as your number one relationship which you pray to, thank, ask forgiveness, seek help from in troubled times, gives you peace, provide a pathway to eternal life, etc? Does your god do this for you?

Maybe you need to re-read these last couple paragraphs? I personally think this is pretty deep stuff; feel I am in unchartered waters and have no real understanding of other gods. Whatever your belief is, just know I am trying to relate with other human beings here who I suspect 'do' have other gods.

So back to my book, my story, my faith and my God. This book is about what I came to realize after some lifetime trials and struggles. This realization recently led me to think, write about and now speak to a set of eight principles shared in my book,

'SIGNIFICANCE Starts Now – How We Live Our Lives Matters'.

1. PEACEFULNESS

2. SERVICE

3. FORGIVENESS

4. THANKFULNESS

5. LEARNING

6. TRANSPARENCY

7. RELATIONSHIP / LOVE

8. FRUITFULNESS

NOTE: If interested in that book?
www.bookertraining.com/2-html or go to Amazon.com.

From the cover of that book, I used these words:

> This book is about YOU.
> It is also about ME.
> It is about PEOPLE, SOCIETY & CULTURE.
> It is about all those around US.
> ...our CHILDREN, our RELATIONSHIPS,
> FAMILY, and your daily walk and lifelong journey.
>
> It is about how WE live this life substantively,
> with purpose with SUCCESS and yes SIGNIFICANTLY!

The book you now hold in your hands (Triangles, Compasses & GOD) is about all that *significance* as well. However this will more specifically focus on YOU on a much more personal level. This is about your survival...

The principles from 'SIGNIFICANCE Starts Now', I learned in much greater depth than ever before as I completed that book and prepared for this one.

Those eight principles along with the soon-to-be-shared 'realized relationship' are the path I have chosen to follow. Clearly I remain a flawed human being, failing to be perfect much of the time. I am trying mind you; this book is part of that trying.

1

LIFE: Who helps?

"So do not fear, for J am with you; do not be dismayed, for J am your God. J will strengthen you and help you; J will uphold you with my righteous right hand..."

Isaiah 41:10

You and I know life indeed challenges us in various ways at various points in time. These challenges may vary from 'minor inconveniences or setbacks' to 'extreme life-impacting devastations'. The central theme I am focusing on here is how and with whom we struggle through life's challenges.

- Where do we find the strength to endure?

- How do we make sense of what is going on, why things are happening or how to accept?

- How do we endure in a peaceful mode without pulling our hair out and going crazy?

- How do we maintain a spirit of 'IT DOESN'T GET ANY BETTER THAN THIS' when we indeed know it does get better than this?

- How do we smile at life and keep on practicing those SIGNIFICANCE principles in the midst of struggles?

- How do we enjoy the journey when it's tough?

- Who, what, how…?

What are we speaking of here, what sorts of struggles? Just posing here some scenarios for clarification.

BIGGEE(s): Divorce, losing a child, bankruptcy, death, chronic illness personally or with loved ones/friends, betrayal, job loss, desperation, hopelessness, addiction, homelessness, abuse on some level.   Maybe we are even talking about someone enslaved, a POW or really trauma-stuff here; on the battlefield, starving literally, rape, murder or some other unimaginable tragedy of life… You get it huh, big stuff!

TOUGHIE(s): Maybe it's just one of those challenges such as: temporarily away from family, non-life threatening hospitalization or illness taking you from work you cannot afford to be missing. Possibly it is about a missing critical resource from your life: a car to get wherever; rent you cannot pay for; or significant financial issues. Possibly a friend in a struggle that is tearing you apart because you cannot take their pain away. Tough stuff for sure, maybe desperate yes, but not life threatening…

INCONVENIENCE-LEVEL STUFF: Seemingly trivial (in comparison with BIGGEEs or TOUGHIEs) as a cold or flu but, a breaking down, your cell phone on the blink, your plumbing backed up and your water cut off temporarily, etc. Maybe it's about a breakup of a relationship – got a dear john letter and you are torn up. Something much larger than a 'bad hair day' but still small in comparison. Just any kind of 'headache' of life that makes 'normal ...well tough'.

NOTE: Let me just say here that as you perused these categories above, you may see some in seemingly the wrong category. Maybe you see the ending of a relationship as being in the TOUGHIE category. I get it. We all connect to the struggles we have had and place different levels of emphasis on them.

Regardless of the struggle, what this is all about is the supporting relationships in our lives that make it possible to handle or not.

- Who do we allow to help us?

- Do they really help us?

- Do they know how or do they do it badly?

- Where and with whom do we find the support?

- Whose shoulder is available for you to pout, cry, whine or totally fall apart on...?

This reminds me of Dave Ramsey the financial guru who makes the point about how many of us seek financial advice from broke people (family, friends, etc)! In this same sense, we likely all do this in various ways in our life; seeking counsel and/or friendship from those who cannot or are not really qualified to do so.

Whoever they are - those that you have 'always' just assumed you will be able to count on; may not be (in reality) always be able to *be there* for you when you really need them.

———————

As I write this, my father has just passed away after mom died only months ago. Likely he figured they would both be there for the other one when illness hit or death was imminent? He was there for Mom, but mom was the first to go. Rut-roh, guess whose 'always' wasn't there for Dad?

Moving on... If you haven't experienced this yet, you will at some point in time. It is inevitable because we humans are not mortal to begin with; he/she cannot always be there. They may have their own challenges happening; preventing them from being there for you. They may be clueless how to help or even downright bad at it – that Dave Ramsey thing again.

Maybe when it hits, your support system has disappeared. Maybe your parents (or that family member or friend) are now gone. You just have no one to go to – to help you process it all, cry on his/her shoulder or from whom to seek some level of support.

That's a scary reality (having no one). It is a reality I fear many in this world exist within!

Unless you fall into one of these 'previously discussed' dynamics right now – you are feeling pretty thankful huh?

Go ahead and give thanks; but you *know* that your time is coming, it's just how life works. I would guess you either just came out of something or unfortunately one may be headed your way. That's life – that 'peaks and valleys' deal, huh?

Q: Who do you have in that role right now?

Point in fact: In some way on some level, somehow, he (she/they/them) or IT will not always be there; I'm just sayin'...

IT?

Well maybe your dependency is (was) not on someone but maybe on your material possessions, maybe your money, savings or finances (it). Maybe all of a sudden that is gone...

This 'realization' of mine provides with absolute certainty, someone *will* be there.

I am so glad I realized what I did before recent times (such as both of my parents passed away this year). I can tell you as I have told many over recent weeks; I had GRIEF WITH PEACE. Dealing with that loss of not only parents but my best friends was doable only because of the 'realization' I am speaking of here. I had peace from my number one relationship in my life. That same peace I did not have during many earlier trials in my life.

Let's just put it this way to wrap this point up: something is going on under the surface with all of us; it may be physical, health, relational, social, financial, etc. Regardless we all have burdens and struggles and need someone(s) to be there for us, with us.

OK so let's get on with it, what's the bottom line here Booker?

2

A Messenger I Believe it Was

"For by grace you have been saved through faith. And this is not your own doing; it is the gift of God, not a result of works, so that no one may boast..."
Ephesians 2:8

Despite the fact I am about to unpack and share some very personal pieces of my life with you; please know this is not done to gain your pity, sympathies or empathy here.

First of all it was a lifetime ago now and I am now 'so good' (and appreciative of the journey) I can't even begin to tell you. Additionally as it all played out, this story turned out to be undoubtedly the significant moment of my life; happening at that very moment. Significantly in a positive way, really!

So anyway, there I was in the midst of my 'not first' divorce - but surely my last. Last undoubtedly because God is clearly in this one (marriage) in His proper place; and she (my wife Sydney) in hers.

*Please know that nothing here is to degrade or otherwise 'put down' a previous relationship, spouse or marriage. Nothing here is about them.

Anyway without going into it ALL, things were bad. Bankruptcy, divorce, essentially homeless-ness, losing my kids a distinct possibility, being disowned by parents (deservedly) for hugely bad choices and decisions made: just some of the dynamics making life very difficult. Not my finest hour, but then again...

This was maybe just prior to the year 2000. I could likely figure out exactly when, but I am not really interested in thinking back through all those bad memories, details, bad choices & decisions to figure it out for you. It doesn't matter.

A reminder here, don't feel badly for me, this was all a very good thing unfolding after all. As I think about it just now, what happened then was tied to the title of my last book, 'SIGNIFICANCE Starts Now'. Our life can change and become significant starting at any moment in time, I believe. More on that point later.

I was in the midst of a boatload of stuff, not knowing what to do or where to turn. It was then when I crossed paths with this guy who was also an insurance salesman. Seeking anyone with some kind or any kind of solution (or hope), I invited him to my home. As the conversation developed he quickly divulged he was 'also' a minister. I am sure he quickly ascertained I needed ministry more than I needed insurance. He was right. Maybe in actuality I got both as it all turned out if you know what I mean.

The faith part of me makes me believe he knew because God had sent him. I don't know this for a fact; it is just what I believe occurred at that moment of time. I must have been so obviously miserable. I know I was, and desperate. He knew that much I am sure.

With the soon-to-be 'ex' lurking around, he laid out some words and thoughts that were taking hold of this desperate soul (me). I cannot tell you all he said, but the single impacting dynamic he shared (which is the root of this message to you) was explained in this simple diagram:

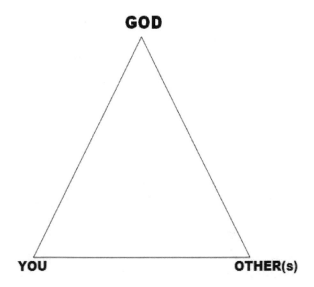

Whether you have a spouse, wife, husband or partner (or don't) this is going to apply to you and stuff in your world.

Let's just say this guy's name was Ronnie (cause it was); he would share a few pieces of thought that have stuck with me to this day. Much of that conversation is the essence of this book you are reading. I would ask you to consider this ALL carefully in YOUR journey moving forward.

Ronnie continued, explaining that if it is all working 'right', this is what should be going on in your worldly and eternal relationships:

<u>* Study the diagram above as you read these:</u>

✓ God must be in the top spot. God must be the #1 relationship above anyone else in your life (the line between YOU and GOD).

✓ If that #1 relationship is real, living, growing and 'right', you are moving up that line toward God. You are getting closer to Him.

✓ You and the OTHER (your spouse maybe) must both have this relationship. Just as you have the line between YOU and GOD and He is your #1 relationship; so must she have the same thing going on?

✓ In both of you focusing first of all on God and continuing to build on that relationship, it has both of you actually moving up the triangle toward Him.

✓ As you both move upward together, you both (you and spouse) are actually coming closer together yourselves! Kind of cool huh?

✓ UN-COOL: If YOU are moving upward and SPOUSE isn't (the other isn't moving upward toward God or maybe isn't even about God) - you and the other are actually moving farther away from each other. Rut-roh...

"Anyone who loves their father or mother more than me is not worthy of me; anyone who loves their son or daughter more than me is not worthy of me. Matthew 10:37

Do these dynamics of the triangle make sense? Picture the different possibilities of one or both moving, neither moving, etc. Study this for a moment; maybe several moments, days, weeks or maybe for the rest of your life?!?

This is important. Until this awareness and buy-in sets in, you cannot BE all you can be spiritually with your god?

...with your spouse...

OK, so back to me, back then, at that point in time several years back. If I am being honest, I do not know whether she (the spouse) was a believer in God or not. For myself, I was not really I don't believe.

What I would discover over time beginning right there and then, was I knew about God, but did not know God. I believe this to be true of many people. He and I did not have a relationship. We had an 'unrealized' relationship maybe, I am not sure. God and Jesus was a concept I heard and I guess *learned* about in church during my upbringing; and adult life in and out of churches.

That relationship with that spouse was a done deal; enough said. As I climbed out of disaster-ville over coming weeks, months and years, I would begin this 'realized' relationship with God.

In just a couple of sentences or so let me share where it all really began to take hold for me – this new relationship (and the one this book is about).

I fairly quickly began a friendship and dialogue with this minister. For about the next 3, 4 or 5 months I was at his home in his office sitting across from him talking and dialoguing about God, the bible, the Word and oh yeah, Jesus – the soon-to-be relationship.

In our times and studies, Ronnie would facilitate my questions, thoughts, ideas and investigation. He would look things up on bible.com or something like that, on his computer and reflect back thoughts, scriptures, meanings and answers. It was one day in the midst of one of these talks when it hit me, "Ahhhhhhhhhhhhhh, so what this is all about is *really* accepting and (in my Leadership terminology) 'buying into' the FACT that there is really a Jesus Christ. He really was the Son of God ...really came down and ...really was crucified for our sins. Oh yeah, and He really returned to be with the Eternal Father..."

Up until this very point in time, I just kind of thought about it all as a neat story, concept or well I don't even know. Maybe the fact is I just never really studied or thought about it that deeply. Maybe it just took a time in my life where I was ready to think about it, when I had no other answers or 'any one' with answers. I will not pretend to tell you I know or understand when or how all these events happen with each of us. Why do I get it and why doesn't he? Is there a chosen dynamic to all this?

- Who gets Saved?
- Born again?
- He found Me?
- I found Him?
- Why doesn't everyone get this...?
- Why did I choose to believe and she didn't?

These are concepts of God and it makes sense to me that I don't and won't ever understand it all. If I could I would be Him huh? That makes sense to me.

Continuing on here; what about those not yet in a relationship with Him? Will they ever be? I am not here to solve that for us; just to share my story and what I believe is or ought to become your story – your God.

THE relationship had begun. Being transparent with you here, from that point in time, it would take at least another five years or so before I really began to change. I believed in Jesus and slowly began talking to Him all the time; and still do. Until just a few years back, I still had not exactly placed Him in the place of honor on the triangle however. He was not THE absolute relationship of my life. The triangle still needed to be understood, realized and practiced.

3

A Talk about My Changing

"*You are the light of the world. A town built on a hill cannot be hidden. Neither do people light a lamp and put it under a bowl. Instead they put it on its stand, and it gives light to everyone in the house. In the same way, let your light shine before others, that they may see your good deeds and glorify your Father in heaven.*"
Matthew 5:14

...the following is a story written a while back; about a speech I did at a Leadership conference... I hope you will put some thought into why I added this to the book, in this spot in the book, etc?...

Dinner was outstanding. The Power & Light District and this place were hits with all in attendance. Plates had been taken away, coffee had been served; some were still picking at their desert. Seeing the Master of Ceremony (MC) moving toward the stage, everyone twisted in their seats or moved their chairs completely around to face the stage.

Raul, one of the breakout facilitators and tonight's MC broke in, "Hope dinner was satisfactory?" He paused knowing he would get plenty of acknowledgements and agreement to that question. "We have a bit of a change with our evening. Pastor Emmanuel, who was to be our speaker, has suffered some kind of serious health issue, we aren't sure yet, maybe even a heart attack. We don't know all the details, but please keep him in your prayers. Sorry for the change, but being leaders, we are sure you can handle change, right?

We are also sure you will not be disappointed with his stand-in. He is someone you have already met and well, from personal experience, I can assure you will indeed enjoy the message. I will just stop and turn it over to my own boss and friend, Booker!"

All began to applaud and looked to the right seeing him step up to the stage and begin walking across. He waved to them smiling big as usual. As he closed in on the podium, the house lights gradually dimmed. The petite candles on the tables and shadow lights on the walls created a pretty cool ambience. He placed his finger to his lips, "shhhhhh..."

As the applause settled and quiet became the only sound, he stood completely motionless and began, "He awakened, this close friend of mine, shivering even though covered by two or three blankets. These were some very tough times for him. Life had bottomed out, he had very little money, a wardrobe pretty much completely from the

Thrift stores he routined, skipping meals to save money for gas, etc.

Anyway, it was middle of the night, and he was in a run-down concrete fishing cabin on Table Rock Lake in central Missouri. It wasn't much due to his current lot in life, but it was home temporarily; the most he could afford. It was late October, nearly Halloween, with winter approaching. It was going to be a hard winter; a fair amount of snow had already fallen that month. As it turned out, he would be stranded much of that winter in this little place in the Ozarks. He would discover before this season was over, this might not be such a bad thing in some ways.

Yes, cold weather was settling in, and he was driving this piece of junk pickup truck with four bald tires. The cabin sat in a deep valley in a southern fork on the lake; very few people remained there over the cold weather months. The cabin had little heat, except for a fireplace and a couple of cheap space-heaters he had picked up at the Salvation Army store. My friend was one of those who actually loved the whole outdoors scene......fireplace, hauling wood, cutting wood and all that he enjoyed. He had a love of the outdoors, wintertime, birds and critters; sitting by the fireplace and all that sort of thing. It was kind of a neat setting, even if he was flat broke with little idea how he would ever recover. The cabin set by the lake shore maybe only fifty meters away. This was a cool situation he figured. *Cool* really didn't describe what it turned out to be there, it was downright cold; he would tell you that if he were here!

Keeping wood on that fire day and night was important. I can still picture his description; he would go to bed with a stocking cap and lots of clothes on and covered up with anything he could. He would have to get up at least once most every night to stoke the fire, throw another log on the fire…you get the picture.

Let me tell you right about now he would be telling you that this is not intended to sound like a sob story. This is not a sad story; in fact this story has much more significance to all this than *my*…. ah, ahem, I mean *his* struggles and troubles at that time."

Booker stopped and momentarily stepped back from the podium, pausing and staring off. There was an awkward moment of silence with people in the audience looking around questioningly at each other.

Just then, with a grin, he returned to the podium offering, "Alright, I've let the cat out of the bag haven't I? Maybe you were already suspecting it; please forgive me for trying to deceive you. This is actually my own personal story I have been describing. Who I have been talking about was me about a decade ago."

After some laughter, chuckling, applause and amen's, he continued on, "So let me tell you the rest of the story, as ol' Paul Harvey would put it.

This was one of the very worst and yet very best times in my life. On the human side, I had huge struggles happening; but on the God side, well…I had found Him. I had found Jesus you see, I was a new man!" Again, another round of amen's and applause took hold. There was all that, but a respectable silence also settled over the room of maybe 90 or so folks in attendance.

"At least now as I look back, I am very sure it was indeed one of the very best periods of my life," Booker was smiling. "I love to share this story. So much has changed and I have learned so much since those days, and I have been so very blessed....amazingly so.

Anyway, that winter I spent my time engulfed in reading the bible, writing a book I had begun, staying warm, walking along the shoreline, and actually fishing for my meals now and then. I love fishing but for sure not very adept at it I must tell you.

Another interesting thing happened during this period; some serious arthritis had somewhat suddenly settled into my hips. I had for the previous 20 years or so, been big into running, long distance races, marathons, triathlons, and all that sort of thing. Running and exercise was critical to my life, dealing with stress, staying physically in shape, working out, etc. I think to this day, that that...getting arthritis, which shut down my running, was God saying 'no you are not going to run away from *this*'. I really think He wanted me focused on Him and our relationship. Whether that is what was happening or not, I am not sure, but will always believe that He shut me down in that regard. I really felt like an old man, and only in my early 40s! I even bought a cane at one point in there. I had no money to go to the doctor. All is good now - that relationship with Him and my hips as well; I had my hips both replaced in 2006. Just running toward him these days!

Now let me take you backward in time a bit, about nine months prior to that winter. It was somewhere around the year 2000 and I was in the midst of a disastrous marriage, bankruptcy and generally bottoming out in life. For the record, I am indeed now in my last marriage and it is an amazing one. I know that's because the Good Lord is in my life now. He led me to a great Believer and lady, my wife Sydney. She sits right over there", pointing down to his left for people to spot her.   She momentarily stood and waved at the audience.

"Anyway, things were really bad, very bad in every regard personally. I had met this insurance salesman, and invited him over to listen to what he had. His name, which I will never forget was Ronnie Black. After just moments sitting at the kitchen table, he revealed he was a minister, as well as an insurance salesman. To this day, I have little doubt that the Good Lord put Ronnie in my life for a reason. We ended up spending the next hour or so talking about the pain in my life.

"As I mentioned this earlier, and no, I didn't know it at the time, this was the best year of my life up to that point. For the next maybe three to five months I spent a couple of nights a week at Ronnie's home sitting in his office while we explored the WORD, Jesus Christ, what the bible said and God. Well, within that next year or so, I moved many times, from Jonesboro, Arkansas to Memphis, to Table Rock Lake, and more, thus the story I just shared.

Somewhere in the midst of all those talks, discussions and exploring, I finally came to understand, that all *this* was simply about actually believing in the fact that there was a JESUS CHRIST who really did come down to earth and really did die on a cross for our sins. To me, this is the Way and the Truth, what I believe anyway.

I can still vividly remember one evening sitting exploring with Ronnie in his office, when that happened and I got it. I was a Believer and one of those *saved* folks. I was new and asked Jesus to forgive my sins and let me into

His Kingdom. This whole *being saved* thing had always seemed weird to me...but it doesn't now.

So, that's enough of my story. Thanks for letting me share it with you.

And now so we can get out of here at some point tonight, let me quickly share what you actually came for tonight, the Reverend's message, titled GOD KNOWS LEADERSHIP.

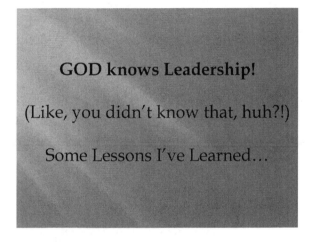

GOD knows Leadership!

(Like, you didn't know that, huh?!)

Some Lessons I've Learned...

Okay, so here are these five ideas that Pastor Immanuel was going to cover with you tonight. That first part was just me taking advantage of you guys and witnessing my story while I had you...pretty sneaky. huh?

This is his stuff, but trust me it's good and powerful. Bear with me and I will try to convey it to you as best I can. I am going to essentially just share this with you straight through, and we'll deal with any questions or thoughts at the end."

He nods to the back of the auditorium for the audio visual person to move to the first slide.

> "...Blessed is the man who finds wisdom; the man who gains understanding."
> PROVERBS 3:13
>
> "...He who loves discipline loves knowledge, he who hates correction is stupid..."
> PROVERBS 12:1

"What is wisdom anyway? As we think of it in regard to leadership, likely many believe it to be centered on how the product(s) is made or how we provide our service(s). Since there are many in management who totally know the product/service, but still struggle in leading their people effectively – doesn't it have to be something more?

Is it just about the business and operational know-how, or could it be something different? I believe it is undoubtedly about all of it - the knowledge of the business, people skills, human behavior/nature, process/systems-thinking, group dynamics and even some organizational development *stuff* thrown in...! Think about it, if you knew about all that and practiced it in your role as a leader, you would likely have to be a pretty amazing leader?

Leaders frequently believe they are *there*, they have arrived. Therefore they must *know it all* ...or at least more than those they lead. If that is so, how do I use that knowledge, that wisdom in leadership? Do I share it, teach it to others, keep it to myself, or just use it to make all the decisions myself?

I always have to be careful in challenging managers, people like all of us here...you guys! Remember, this is not about anyone being bad, but just about bad management and leadership practices maybe.

The scriptures up there encourage us to find and discover wisdom, maybe above anything else. Again, I ask you to consider here, 'what is leadership wisdom; what do leaders need to know'? Hopefully you found some answers today and will find even more of those answers tomorrow.

Along with our own understanding, opinions and beliefs in this matter, we should seek the input of others around us. We should identify; work on our leadership competencies and ask others to help us with our learning journey. We need to be okay with those and their input when they do point out things or challenge us when we are falling short. Wisdom would tell us that old phrase, 'two heads are better than one' is a truism.   A lack of wisdom would cause the leader to not ask other's opinions or to reject feedback from others."

Smiling and pausing for a moment to let people think, he looked toward the back for the next slide, "Here's our second point."

"...Now before the feast of the Passover, when Jesus knew that his hour was come that he should depart out of this world unto the Father; having loved his own which were in the world, he loved them unto the end..."
JOHN 13:1

"There's a lot there isn't there? Some pretty heavy stuff. We hear from many leaders, '...don't get too close to your people. There's a fine line to be kept between you and your people ...keep your distance ...you can't be a friend and a boss.'

These are commonly spoken and widely accepted management myths heard when people speak of the workplace and a manager's relationship with his or her people. Managers say those things maintaining the status quo.   Just possibly real leaders know it is just management-speak. The leader grows, builds & improves these relationships and all relations continually! Real leaders know their success depends on the quality of these relationships.

Because so many people have seen this fine line-concept necessary due to past manager's abusing their authority and position; it has come to be accepted in management circles. It is found in management-theory courses and most anyplace you see management taught. However, we here agree with the pastor on this, we don't buy it for a second. We are teaching leadership and relationship here at the Great Eight Conference. You've already witnessed some of that in today's sessions haven't you?

We believe this mentality comes from bad experiences where untrained managers, not leaders practiced favoritism, abused their roles, not holding all equally accountable, taking advantage of people, promoting on friendship, and so on.

If you are a leader or trying to become one, realize this. If your attempts at leadership have been less than productive, very likely this is at the root of your problems.

Your success is going to come from them, your people, and those relationships. What kind of leader would YOU perform for the best? What leader have YOU worked for the most effectively? Of course the answer is the one you had the best relationship with, right? We speak of the importance of relationships among team members and how dysfunctional teams are when relationships aren't good. But then we suggest the leader needs to keep his or her distance? What kind of illogical nonsense is that I ask you?

Don't fall into that way of thinking; work on developing relationships with your folks as tightly as possible. When you create comfort, trust, respect, great communications and a desire for people to want to be there with YOU and the others......great things can and will happen. When you and the team have great relationships all the way around, these are where the good stories come from. The result is awesome productivity, loyalty, low turnover and believe it or not, people looking forward to coming to work ...and maybe even being willing to stay late! When the leader cares about his or her folks ...when the leader is there for them outside their job ...when the leader wants to support, listen and help them with troubles ...and yes even socializes with them ....now we have a great family-like work environment.

Now of course, there are issues and risks to be understood; but not if YOU the leader do things right! If fair expectations and accountability happen with everyone, these issues don't exist! The problem is NOT about this buddy and boss concept and debate; it's about YOU the leader, and your leadership! I have indeed worked with and coached great leaders who would not go there as I am describing! They maintained this fine line and wouldn't let the relationship exist past it. It's just my opinion they were limiting themselves & the potential of this relationship. They were creating a barrier to further good stuff happening. They have created a boundary and limit to any further being achieved as the leader there possibly.

Jesus broke bread and spent countless hours teaching, socializing & continuously improving the relationships with those he led. The Word speaks to developing a personal relationship with HIM. Shouldn't the most ultimate leader's leadership be our guide, think about it?"

Lots of amen's and applause from various parts of the room followed. He allowed for a couple of follow-up comments to be made quickly before giving the nod to the audiovisual technician...

> "…therefore I tell you, do not worry about life, what you will eat or drink; or about your body, what you will wear. Who of you by worrying can add a single hour to his life? O ye of little faith! Your Heavenly Father knows what you need. Seek first His Kingdom and righteousness and all these things will be given to you. Therefore do not worry about tomorrow."
> MATTHEW 6:25-34

"Let's continue on so I can get you folks out of here sometime tonight. Our third point of the pastor's is important guys. Not worrying is a tough concept for all of us humans, no matter who you are! Leaders have to deal with this personally …as well as for those they lead! That's leadership we're talking about here, not managers who think people should leave their worries at the front door!

In these challenging times with so much hurting, hopelessness, bad economy; people, folks losing jobs, business struggling, oil spilling, tornados, tsunamis, earthquakes, disasters here and there, people laid off …who or what is next? Will it be you, a loved one or some of those you lead? It is nearly a daily occurrence to hear from someone close in our lives who have been hit by something negative right? I heard from a good friend and executive just this morning that is now out of a job; then hearing that they just discovered cancer in her body. Problems and concerns are everywhere, and we're not supposed to worry?!? Indeed, this is one of the tougher biblical principles we are supposed to follow… Yikes, I mean double yikes."

Booker paused, grabbing his water for a sip. He then went on, "As leaders we are *really* needed by those we lead. As much as we may want to focus & dwell on our own worries, stresses and problems ...your folks need you and your leadership! A few points to share as I have been pondering this much lately myself, and with my own team here at the conference.

First off, let them know you also have concerns personally, as well as your concern for them. Be human, be real, and don't be afraid of letting them see it. When we let others in ...we build trust and strong relationships. Some believe this shows weakness as a leader, that's not only wrong, but stupid. That's just my opinion, mind you."

"The relationships in our lives make tough times much more palatable; especially when one of those relationships is his or her boss ...our boss even! When we all get through these times, which we will, unless we don't..." he paused momentarily smiling at all. "Things will turn around, but in the meantime trusting relationships you built with them will pay huge dividends.

Relationships between co-workers can become very strained as individuals withdrawal, focus and concentration dims, and/or people lashing out at others. Don't avoid it or try to pretend stress is not there. It is real and everyone feels it. Why not get it out for all to know and realize that we are all dealing with it. You the leader and the rest of the team are there for each other. It needs to be be dealt with, exposed and curtailed before it gets out of hand. Although we can never be sure of our security (of our jobs) and those that we lead, we need to reassure our people as much as possible; and with the truth as we know it!

You may be thinking that you are not there to be a counselor, therapist or psychologist! I for one totally disagree. Real leaders are absolutely those things; they are conscious and realize that their job is indeed all of these and more. It may not be in your job description, but trust me, the ones you lead know what they need from you."

Without pause he pointed to the back, to the audiovisual technician, who was way ahead of him.

> "…You have heard, 'Love your neighbor and hate your enemies.' But I tell you, 'Love your enemies and pray for those who persecute you, that you may be sons of your Father in Heaven.' If you love those who love you, what reward will you get? Even the tax collectors do that. And if you greet only your brothers, what are you doing better, or more, than others?…"
> MATTHEW 5:43

"Number four here tonight. This scripture has particular significance to all of us in the workplace, just as in every part of our lives. This reminds me of something I wrote a few years ago regarding working with others. The article focused on the challenge of working with those we don't get along with …those we are in conflict with …or let's just say the relationship is less than good! Loving those with whom we work can be tough, but we are called to do so. Maybe HE would accept us just *liking* them and getting along with these others?

We all have these people in our lives from time to time. The correct response should be to address them as quickly as possible to get that stress out of our lives. For me, in my leadership preaching and teaching, it is about the insanity of working side by side with a bad relationship ...day after day after day after day. It's like that Groundhog Day movie, out a while back, every morning he woke up and faced exactly the same day, dynamics, relationships, issues, etc. I believe we just become numb and unconscious of the stupidity of this. We lose focus on just how much they are impacting us and those around us, and them."

Leaders are really needed in these situations. We are the ones responsible to be watching for these conflicts, issues and what we refer to around here as bottlenecks.

Yes, the personal leadership of solving these relationships not just in your life, but also those folks you supervise in the workplace. He, she, they need you to get involved and facilitate real resolution. You are needed to get them out of this insanity, when they can't or won't by themselves.

The reality is that we must deal with these relationships - it is your job! For the record, it is always your business, no matter the circumstances! Why? ...because people in conflict, to some degree have to be negatively impacting productivity, communications, relationships, morale...

How you do it may seem challenging, however the first step is to be committed and persist in not letting them exist on your team. That's what you are paid the big bucks for, isn't it? We'll be giving you some tips and strategies on this in our breakout sessions by the way.

As you begin to hesitate or procrastinate about taking action with any of this; remember that HE, as in Matthew 5:43, up there on the wall ...directs us to do so."

He was smiling at them with an inquisitive look on his face and nodding for the last time for his last slide.

> "When they saw Jesus having dinners with tax collectors and 'sinners,' they asked his disciples, 'Why does your teacher eat with them'? On hearing this, Jesus said, 'It is not the healthy who need a doctor, but the sick. Go and learn what this means....
> For I have not come for the righteous, but sinners and the sick.'"
> MATTHEW 9:11-13

"So here's the last one for tonight. There are so many messages within these scriptures up here, for leaders. Allow me to focus on one I relate to a lot, one I use in discussions with leaders. First off, here's an assumption from my first book if I may...

'Both leaders and followers in the workplace and our society have become accepting and numb to ineffective leadership. Most of us have accepted how non-productive, unenthusiastic, and ineffective management and our quote teams ...and those around us really are! We accept this as just the way it is and poor relationships between individuals and departments, conflicts and bottlenecks, poor attitudes, bad apples and bad management, ...are just part of the landscape'.

The point I make a lot is regarding this *bad-apples* thought. There is this conscious or subconscious thinking on the part of many in leadership roles, ...that there just will always be a couple of bad apples on any team. These bad apples might be viewed as the two or three folks on every team that have issues, life problems, ...they cause trouble, ... they challenge you and others all the time, ...don't seem to be team-players, ... the ones always in conflict,... or some other shortcoming. You are picturing someone right now aren't you?" Booker smiled, actually strolling across the stage to the other side, then continuing on.

"In looking back at the scripture, Jesus speaks of HIS role to teach, serve lead, heal and teach! The righteous or healthy ones, the other eighty percent or whatever of those on your team, are not who need your leadership. It's the bad apples. Leaders tend to take credit for the eighty percent, and use the bad-apple excuse to avoid their job as the leader ...there is where the real leadership challenge is. Likely the other eighty just really require any ol' knucklehead manager!

Managers & organizations often just view these bad apples as if they are unsalvageable; the only solution is to just get rid of them. While there is undoubtedly a small percentage that deserve this and need to be tossed out, ...the vast majority in my humble opinion, can be led to become healthy productive team players.

Are you up for your leadership challenge, to go back and fix those bad apples you have been using as an excuse? Are you willing to have dinners with the sick, those in need;

to teach and make them well? Jesus knew his purpose. Do you, do we, and does organizational leadership get this …not many I'd say. What say you?"

Booker was headed back to the podium, grabbed his water, acknowledged a few commentaries and offered, "That's it, some pretty good food for thought from our sick friend I'd say. I hope you find it ties in with all your learning today and tomorrow…. We better get out of here gang. I want you fresh for some more learning tomorrow. Don't forget, if interested we have a short church service planned in the morning. If you didn't know or you want some information, check with us on the way out of here. Go enjoy a nice stroll back to the hotel in the great Kansas City weather going on out there."

*Shared previously in my 3rd book on Leadership, 'The Conference for Leaders'
People were beginning to rise and applauding enthusiastically. He excitedly motioned for them to stop, which they did after a few moments.

Most remained standing, turning back toward Booker. "Thank you for that. Before we go, let me end this with a challenge to you to share *your* story with others! This is not a matter of imposing on others. We are charged to witness to others, to bring others to know about our God. So as I have done with you tonight, you are accountable to start sharing yours. Now, that's obviously up to each one of us. God's very best to each of you, thanks again for coming tonight. I'll be around here for a bit and of course all day tomorrow at the conference. Don't forget church in the morning if interested." All again rose and clapped as he clicked off the podium light, gathered his notes and bottle of water, heading down the stairs to mingle. He did so until nearly 11:15 pm that night.

4

Who (What) occupies
Your Triangle

"And God spoke all these words: 'I am the LORD your God, who brought you out of Egypt, out of the land of slavery…   You shall have no other gods before me.

You shall not make for yourself an image in the form of anything in heaven above or on the earth beneath or in the waters below. You shall not bow down to them or worship them…" Exodus 20

Let me offer up a challenge for you here. Maybe it's time to really ponder where you are with all this. This is all about YOU, that one on the bottom left of the triangle.

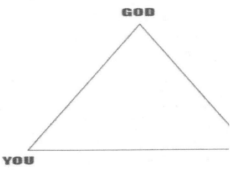

Notice the bottom-right corner (point) of the triangle is left out (intentionally).

Let's begin. First of all, who is in *your* top spot? My message to you and my belief is that if it is anything or anyone but God, life will be a struggle full of disappointments until that dynamic changes. People will:

- Let you down
- They will go away
- They will die
- They will betray
- They will make mistakes
- They will be unavailable
- They cannot be all you will need them to be…
- They will not be Him (GOD)…

- Mom will let Dad down (she passed away)… My parents both died, thus not being there for me now… One day my wife will not be there (or I won't be there for her)…

When all this came clear for me, I suddenly was brought into a consciousness that He is the only one who will never do any of these things above. He and our relationship will 'always' be there for me.

Let me present another perspective of all this for us to ponder (actually I already did☺).

The bottom right point on the triangle maybe isn't a *significant other* in the sense we have been discussing here. Maybe it's a thing - a possession or some other material *thing*? Maybe it's your lifestyle, your routine, your finances, your material objects, your kids, hobby, home, etc…

The diagram that follows here is simply there to give you a visual to ponder as you think through all this.

Is someone or something else in that top spot, on that pedestal for you? I have just placed possible alternatives in there for you to consider. What is important to you in this life of yours? Maybe another consideration might be **MONEY**!

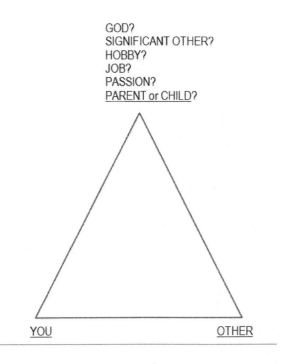

GOD?
SIGNIFICANT OTHER?
HOBBY?
JOB?
PASSION?
PARENT or CHILD?

YOU   OTHER

Let me share with you of a very important piece that fell into place and hit me squarely between the eyes one day. I had not yet understood or embraced this all.

I still was placing others in this top spot! I had not processed, assimilated or otherwise put this all together: God ...the triangle ...YOU and my OTHER ...someone ...Jesus ...other relationship dynamics, etc.

Before I lay this out completely, study the triangle again for another moment or two. Who or what holds that place of honor (the top spot) for you?

Here is what somehow finally struck me and became part of my 'realization' as the learning unfolded. By the way, learning is still underway – I know I have TONS to learn. Here is that piece that fell into place and helped clarify some of this for me.

Ready, here goes...

Bottom line, I was placing my loved ones *there*. Early in life this was my parents who occupied that spot for me. They loved me, gave me stuff, taught me, protected me, they were who I went to when in trouble, etc.

Then later ....get this point - my wife (female relationship, romance or significant other) always was in that spot. Without the relationship with God and Jesus in my life and taking His proper place at the top, I just always placed my spouse there.

It was my mindset that this is how things should be and just seemed right; she was the one I had on that pedestal. That is part of why the triangle hit me so significantly when Ronnie drew it out on our kitchen table. Not only was my spouse not moving with me toward God in that top spot – God wasn't there, only her.

There really wasn't a triangle, but just a straight line over to 'her'; or maybe the line upward toward her (SPOUSE)...where GOD should have been...

NOT REAL SURE.

It was *her* I was idolizing, trying to please, serving - believing to be that one #1 relationship in my world. It seems funny as I think of it now, but I was trying to climb toward her and likely she was trying to get off that pedestal! I won't go further here; I know what you are thinking and well... let's move on. After you get that picture out of your head about 'her' trying to escape, consider the more serious point here about placing anyone or anything but God on that pedestal.

To be very specific here, I am sure placing any one of them on a pedestal was not what any of them wanted. Who can/could live up to being God after all? It was likely part of the dynamic of how I chased mates away on some level during those seasons/years...

Again the point here is that no one of us humans can live up to that spot. Anyone or anything we place *there* just won't work! I hope this makes *some* sense to you here? I have to be honest and tell you this is all getting a bit too complicated and I am not sure where to go from here with this point – so I won't. I will hope and pray the connection, intended understanding and realization is there for you.

It's God-stuff; it *cannot* be easy to grasp it all.

Take what works and fits for you and go work on it all...

While on this point, I would tell you that others have held that God-spot in my life. Consider who has been (is) in that spot for you - parents, teachers, coaches, a peer or mentor?

Again my parents (and likely most parents) hold this for some period of time in a child's life. For sure my parents who I greatly admired and respected were like my God(s) early on in life. This point makes me think of how natural all this is to get screwed up and have others occupying the God-spot.

Who else do we put there - kids?   Yeah, I think of how many parents do this same thing with their kids (seemingly more and more and more these days); 'whatever the kids want' is their mantra. The kid is placed on this pedestal by many parents making the child believe well, some really wrong stuff. We place them there, make everything about them and they go screw it up - because oh yeah, they are not God.

Work, making money or the job is IT for many I fear. Undoubtedly money would be a no-brainer here - holding that spot for many. That idolizing of the almighty dollar I fear sits on that elite spot for many of this world. Maybe it is also could be something like a sport one excels in or is passionate about; a hobby or art someone masters, etc.

You get the point anyway, right?

There is so much of my life that is so much clearer now that God and the Triangle have been 'realized' and/or have gone to another level of learning and understanding.

?   *How leadership (personally and professionally) should work?*

?   *How a marriage should work?*

?   *How any relationship should work?*

?   *How both down below need both be moving up toward Him...?*

5

MODELED in The Walk

"What you have learned, received, heard and seen in me - practice these things, and the God of peace will be with you..."
Philippians 4:9

Maybe just a bit more about the triangle is needed here as we transition to this chapter. For you, me and all of us humans, the leg of the triangle between (YOU) and GOD represents what should be the most important, relevant and perfect relationship that could exist in your world. It becomes what should become your model for all the other relationships in your life.

The best model for a relationship and true friendship is the one God and Jesus Christ portray in the bible. I focus primarily on the New Testament and the Walk of Jesus on this earth. Jesus practiced principles and practiced relationships in that perfect way. There are many lessons I have extracted from Jesus that have vastly improved my walk, thinking and practices in life. This pertains to relationships and also my other passion in life – my work in Leadership.

It is the model for the way we all wish and hope the relationships in our life would be, but rarely are (actually never are perfectly executed). Here I want to just present a few of those practical principles.

What these few principles below answer specifically are these questions:

- ❖ **What is the perfect relationship?**

- ❖ **What makes for the perfect friend or friendship?**

- ❖ **How should we be if we are practicing relationship(s) on the highest level with others?**

Jesus modeled and taught about what a perfect relationship should BE. His *walk*, actions, teachings, behaviors and words demonstrated what we all should seek (in our relationships) and what we should BE.

What follows is just a sampling of relational-perspectives HE demonstrated and what we should strive for among all of us *humans*. These scriptures and quotations are merely here for your pondering and consideration. I want to present and suggest here an over-arching and all encompassing concept of how we should view our relationships. Much of it comes from my personal understanding of what many of us know as the 'Golden Rule'...

'Do unto others as we would have them do unto us'

...which is not necessarily a scriptural finding but is undoubtedly how we are to BE. As you consider these relationship principles below, consider them each in this sense: What if both sides of the relationship were practicing and BE-ing these? Secondly also consider this as I have come to think of what that Golden Rule thing is all about:

'DO UNTO OTHERS AS YOU HAVE
GOD
DO UNTO YOU'

This now takes on a whole other dynamic when we first consider how we should BE! Now I don't believe God is going to be vengeful regarding our shortcomings with others, but will love us unconditionally. I also believe that He wants us to use His model 'that Jesus walked' as our baseline for guiding our relationships.

Do you want God to love you, care for you, forgive you, grant you peace, etc (as these principles cover)? Then how we want to be treated by Him is how we should treat others (which were created by Him you realize huh?) He made all of us in His way.

Consider this scripture; and how we should BE - how we should treat others. Then we will move on for a brief look at some other relationship principles modeled for us by Him...

The Sheep and the Goats (Matthew 25:40)

"When the Son of Man arrives, He will take his place with all the nations arranged before him and he will sort the people out, much as a shepherd sorts out sheep and goats, putting sheep to his right and goats to his left. Then the King will say to those on his right, 'Enter, you who are blessed by my Father! Take what's coming to you in this kingdom. It's been ready for you since the world's foundation. And here's why:

I was hungry and you fed me,
I was thirsty and you gave me a drink,
I was homeless and you gave me a room,
I was shivering and you gave me clothes,
I was sick and you stopped to visit,
I was in prison and you came to me.'

"Then those 'sheep' are going to say, 'Master, what are you talking about? When did we ever see you hungry and feed you, thirsty and give you a drink? And when did we ever see you sick or in prison and come to you?' Then the King will say, 'I'm telling the solemn truth: Whenever you did one of these things to someone overlooked or ignored, that was me—you did it to me.'

"Then he will turn to the 'goats,' the ones on his left, and say, 'Get out, worthless goats! You're good for nothing but the fires of hell. And why? Because—

I was hungry and you gave me no meal,
I was thirsty and you gave me no drink,

*I was homeless and you gave me no bed,
I was shivering and you gave me no clothes,
Sick and in prison, and you never visited.'*

"Then those 'goats' are going to say, 'Master, what are you talking about? When did we ever see you hungry or thirsty or homeless or shivering or sick or in prison and didn't help?'

"He will answer them, 'I'm telling the solemn truth: Whenever you failed to do one of these things to someone who was being overlooked or ignored, that was me—you failed to do it to me.'

"Then those 'goats' will be herded to their eternal doom, but the 'sheep' to their eternal reward." Matt 25:31

❖ **THE PERFECT RELATIONSHIP is reliable and always there for each other.**

Loyal
Dependable
Available
Shoulder to...
Steadiness
Fidelity
Constancy
Devotion
Faithful

For Jesus doesn't change—yesterday, today, tomorrow, he's always totally himself. Hebrews 13:6

"Remember, we all stumble, every one of us. That's why it's a comfort to go hand in hand." Emily Kimbrough

❖ **THE PERFECT RELATIONSHIP is one of giving, service, helpful and supporting of each other.**

Servant heart
Focus on Others
Accommodating
Caring
Lend a hand
Thoughtful
Considerate

"What does it profit, my brethren, if someone says he has faith but does not have works? Can faith save him? If a brother or sister is naked and destitute of daily food, and one of you says to them, "Depart in peace, be warmed and filled," but you do not give them the things which are needed for the body, what does it profit? Thus also faith by itself, if it does not have works, is dead..." James 2:14

"How wonderful it is that nobody need wait a single moment before starting to improve the world."
Anne Frank

❖ **THE PERFECT RELATIONSHIP is one of forgiving and acceptance despite our flaws, imperfections, sins and mistakes.**

Merciful	Tolerant
Pardoning	Empathetic
Lenient	Understand
Sympathetic	Non-judgmental

Peter asked, "Master, how many times do I forgive a brother or sister who hurts me? Seven?"

Jesus replied, "Seven! Hardly. Try seventy times seven.

"The kingdom of God is like a king who decided to square accounts with his servants. As he got under way, one servant was brought before him who had run up a debt of a hundred thousand dollars. He couldn't pay up, so the king ordered the man, along with his wife, children, and goods, to be auctioned off at the slave market.

"The poor wretch threw himself at the king's feet and begged, 'Give me a chance and I'll pay it all back.'

Touched by his plea, the king let him off, erasing the debt.

"The servant was no sooner out of the room when he came upon one of his fellow servants who owed him ten dollars. He seized him by the throat and demanded, 'Pay up. Now!'

"The poor wretch threw himself down and begged, 'Give me a chance and I'll pay it all back.' But he wouldn't do it. He had him arrested and put in jail until the debt was paid. When the other servants saw this going on, they were outraged and brought a detailed report to the king.

"The king summoned the man and said, 'You evil servant! I forgave your entire debt when you begged me for mercy. Shouldn't you be compelled to be merciful to your fellow servant who asked for mercy?' The king was furious and put the screws to the man until he paid back his entire debt. And that's exactly what my Father in heaven is going to do to each one of you who doesn't forgive unconditionally anyone who asks for mercy."
Matthew 18:21

"I can forgive, but I cannot forget. This is only another way of saying, I will not forgive. Forgiveness ought to be like a cancelled note - torn in two, and burned up, so that it never can be shown against one"
Henry Ward Beecher

❖ **THE PERFECT RELATIONSHIP demonstrates a thankful attitude. Appreciative of each other as well as the relationship is of utmost importance.**

Grateful	Indebted
Pleased	Satisfied
Gratified	Acceptance

"Jesus sat down and taught his climbing companions. This is what he said: "You're blessed when you're at the end of your rope. With less of you there is more of God and his rule.

"You're blessed when you feel you've lost what is most dear to you. Only then can you be embraced by the One dearest to you.

"You're blessed when you're content with just who you are—no more, no less. That's the moment you find yourselves proud owners of everything that can't be bought.

"You're blessed when you've worked up a good appetite for God. He's food and drink in the best meal you'll ever eat.

"You're blessed when you care. At the moment of being 'care-full,' you find yourselves cared for.

"You're blessed when you get your inside world—your mind and heart—put right. Then you can see God in the outside world.

"You're blessed when you can show people how to cooperate instead of compete or fight. That's when you discover who you really are, and your place in God's family..." Matt 5:9

?

"One need only to open his eyes for a moment (pause in dwelling on his own problems), look around anywhere and see the struggles, pain and troubles of so many. Upon 'seeing', that feeling arising in you is thankfulness and appreciation that you do not have their troubles. Thankfulness comes only from 'once again' taking the focus from self and onto others; then we see how good we have it. The significantly-thankful individual knows we deserve nothing more than we have at any moment. Give thanks and be thankful daily - and even before you receive..." (Wording used from my book SIGNIFICANCE Starts Now)

❖ **THE PERFECT RELATIONSHIP is one of transparency, truth and sincerity.**

Clearness	Legitimate
Lucid	Genuine
Simplicity	Actual
Fact	Authentic
Certainty	Real
Reality	

"Do not be conformed to this world, but be transformed by the renewal of your mind, that by testing you may discern what is the will of God, what is good and acceptable and perfect. For by the grace given to me I say to everyone among you not to think of himself more highly than he ought to think..." Romans 12:1

"...that we deal with so much internal 'inward poverty' – we doctor up impressions we put out there for others; we artificially present ourselves; we are all so in need of deliverance from 'pretense' in how we live..."
A.W.Tozer

❖ **THE PERFECT RELATIONSHIP loves and always builds on the relationship between each other.**

Admires	Worship
Adores	Devoted
Likes	Fond
Accepts	Irresistible
Wants	Affection

"You're familiar with the old written law, 'Love your friend,' and its unwritten companion, 'Hate your enemy.' I'm challenging that. I'm telling you to love your enemies. Let them bring out the best in you, not the worst. When someone gives you a hard time, respond with the energies of prayer, for then you are working out of your true selves, your God-created selves. This is what God does. He gives his best—the sun to warm and the rain to nourish—to everyone, regardless: the good and bad, the nice and nasty. If all you do is love the lovable, do you expect a bonus? Anybody can do that. If you simply say hello to those who greet you, do you expect a medal? Any run-of-the-mill sinner does that."
Matt 5: 47

?

"Relationship is the key to people succeeding together. Trust and relationship not developed on the front-end of people functioning together will nearly always become a

problem. In my work with leadership, cultures and organizations what many contend are communication issues are (90% of the time I believe) actually relationship issues. Always be creating new ones, building on current ones and fixing damaged relationships."

(ME)

❖ **THE PERFECT RELATIONSHIP cares about one another.**

Interested	Concern
Kindness	Sensitive
Thoughtful	Loving
Considerate	Selfless
Compassionate	Attentive

"A new commandment I give to you, that you love one another: just as I have loved you, you also are to love one another. By this all people will know that you are my disciples, if you have love for one another."
John 13:34

?

"People don't care how much you know until first they know how much you care"

J. Maxwell I believe gets credit...

❖ **THE PERFECT RELATIONSHIP involves clarity with Expectations & Accountabilities.**

Responsible   Answerable
Clarity   Liable
Understood   Transparent
Roles

"*...For we will all stand before God's judgment seat. It is written:*

*'As surely as I live,' says the Lord,
'every knee will bow before me; every tongue will acknowledge God.'*

...so then, each of us will give an account of ourselves to God..."
Romans 14:11

?

"*We must reject the idea that every time a law is broken, society (the organization or culture) is guilty rather than the lawbreaker. It is time to restore the American precept that everyone is accountable for his own actions...*"
Ronald Reagan

❖ **THE PERFECT RELATIONSHIP is one where understanding is sought vs. 'being right' or 'winning'. Listening comes first.**

Understand	Selfless
Perceptive	Concern
Considerate	Discerning
Respect	Observant
Attention	Hearing
Attitude	

*"Listen to advice and accept discipline,
and at the end you will be counted among the wise"*
Proverbs 19:20

*"Seek first to understand before
trying to be understood."*
Stephen Covey

❖ **THE PERFECT RELATIONSHIP does not judge but accepts each other.**

Tolerant	Charitable
Patient	Open-minded
Long-suffering	Generous
Complain (not)	Appreciative

"Do not judge others or you too will be judged. For in the same way you judge others, you will be judged... Why do you look at the speck of sawdust in your brother's eye and pay no attention to the plank in your own eye? How can you say to your brother, 'Let me take the speck out of your eye,' when all the time there is a plank in your own eye..." Luke 6:37

"...when judging a friend, remember that he is judging you with the same godlike and superior impartiality."
Arnold Bennett

"It is a very common human flaw that we tend to judge other's sins and mistakes - in comparison to ours (sins & mistakes). Thus believing theirs to be serious, but ours to be trivial" (ME)

❖ **THE PERFECT RELATIONSHIP grows each other; helps and allows each other to always be learning, changing and improving.**

Learning	Understand
Improving	Insight
Betterment	Intelligence
Wisdom	Worldly
Education	Behavior
Knowledge	

"Get wisdom; get insight; do not forget, and do not turn away from the words of my mouth. Do not forsake her (learning & wisdom), and she will keep you; love her, and she will guard you..." Proverbs 4:5

"All Scripture is breathed out by God and profitable for teaching, for reproof, for correction, and for training in righteousness, that the man of God may be competent, equipped for every good work..." 2 Timothy 3:16

"The purpose of life is not to be happy - but to matter, to be productive, to be useful, and to have it make a difference that you have lived at all."
Leo Rosten

"The absolute best relationships not only include support, caring and someone that will listen – but one where we learn and grow from each other (through honest feedback, critique and advice). Real relationships do not receive critique as an attack but rather accept it as help. After all, our own opinions of ourselves are kind of biased huh?" (ME)

6

Compasses can Break

"If anyone would come after me, he must deny himself and take up his cross daily and follow me..."
(Luke 9:23)

The compass enters the picture here as another way to think about these 'points of the triangle'. Who or what is your compass? What or who provides you direction, clarifies your path, leads the way for you?

I shall use the passing of my parents once again to stress a concept. My mother and father both died this year. They were clearly compasses in my life for those 58 years. Although they taught me much and left me much in regard to life and how to live it; those compasses are now 'broken'. I can no longer seek direction from them; cannot call them for support, advice or counsel. They are not there to console me, encourage me or teach me anything from here on... I never really understood they would actually be gone one day. I believe this happens with many (maybe most) of us: not realizing *they* will at some point in time, not be there!

I can tell you as I write this; I am in a bit of a fog with two of my compasses having broken. Some depression and lost-ness is felt; grief is occurring but I have to tell you there is also plenty of peace and direction. My direction is still very clear because my primary compass is that ONE (God) at the top of my triangle.

Somehow, SAVED or BORN AGAIN never quite
worked for me. I heard this recently & somehow it works for me:

"GRACE found me somehow..."

The peace is from two dynamics:

1) My real #1 compass became and is today Christ, Jesus and God. He was and is always there. He gets me through all this loss of important people from my life.

2) Peace also totally exists *because my relationship with Mom & Dad was excellent as they passed away. We were 'good' with each other – big time 'good'*.

NOTE: ***This is a critically important lesson here - keep your relationships good, right and strong always – you just never know.***

As discussed previously, important people in our lives will go away; they will be a 'compass breaking'. They may have provided direction, assistance and some clarity about things when they were here, but no more.

Inevitably another one of those humans has let us down. Everyone here is human, get it?

By the way, you are a compass for some (or for many) aren't you? What will come of them when you are not there for them? If you are holding that top spot for someone(s), maybe you should help them sort all this out...

We have compasses in our lives from day one. These (people) may be pretty accurate and dependable ones - maybe only a degree off in their 'direction' to us. Whatever their value, if they have not yet become undependable or broken completely, they likely will. None of us can ever be 100% dependable; we're not in control you see? We are not infallible, not 100% reliable – we are human.

As I think about the compass as a direction-finder, it makes me think of other ways we humans attempt to find our way. Stars, fortune tellers, self-declared prophets, sundials, etc – all these are only marginally effective. Each has its own issues and again is not totally reliable ...always!

So what (who) is your compass now? What compasses have steered you in your life? Where are they now; still have one you can count on...totally, 100% always to be there and accurate? Sorry but 'no way Jose'.

People & Relationships: Maybe your compass is a person (parent, spouse, best friend, teacher, etc). They may go away, become unavailable, conflict may set in, they will break a promise ... or they die on you?

Stuff, things, or materialism: Maybe your job was it at some point or what you consider your compass right now? It is what you do and who you are. Possibly it is some other passion – a hobby, sport, riches, a home/yard, possessions, collectibles, etc? Even worse than people - material objects, activities, stuff... WILL not be permanent!

They will eventually dry up, turn to dust/rust or go away for one reason or another.

"You're blessed when you feel you've lost what is most dear to you. Only then can you be embraced by the One dearest to you." Matthew 5:4

7

Not Going Back to Fishing
*like Peter did

"... Jesus revealed himself again to the disciples by the Sea of Tiberius. Simon Peter, Thomas, Nathanael, the sons of Zebedee, and two other disciples of his were together. Simon Peter told them, "I am going fishing." "We will go with you," they replied. They went out and got into the boat, but that night they caught nothing.

When it was already very early morning, Jesus stood on the beach, but the disciples did not know that it was Jesus.

So Jesus said to them, "Children, you don't have any fish, do you? They replied, "No." He told them, "Throw your net on the right side of the boat, and you will find some." So they threw the net, and were not able to pull it in because of the large number of fish..."

John 21:3

[A good friend we will call Charlie (because that's his name) recently led me to this verse for a completely other reason than I am presenting here. Charlie's thought and lesson was a good learning, but I went in a completely different direction with it! It is one of the beautiful things about God, the bible and His Word – it teaches us all different things at different times. At different times we can take a completely different message from the same passage.

This God of mine (ours) knows what He is doing huh? It is like magic how that happens; actually I guess it is just Godly. Again I am OK with not understanding, He is God.]

So back to the point here with this scripture. What it *speaks* to me is how easily it is to go back to where you were before God/Jesus entered your (our) life. Maybe we are not or were not immediately changed. It is where I connect with the phrasing of 'what happens' to us as being Born Again.

When we accept and begin that relationship, we begin learning all over again (as if we were just born). The real learning is yet to come.

In this scripture, Peter and others after Jesus' departure decide to 'go fishing'. Now it may not be what scholars think about this scripture - but for me, it is *powerfully* making the point that we have to be careful not to return to our old ways without Him.

Suddenly He was gone from them...

Without Him they went back to fishing (their old ways) and caught nothing. When He came back into their lives, they caught more fish than they could even handle...

It is so representative to me in regards to what we all do to some degree in much of our daily living. We can be one minute relating closely to God only to turn in the next moment and do some sinful thing (or maybe just attempt something on our own without involving Him). Maybe akin to how some people go to church every Sunday but come Monday revert to un-Christ like ways. They went back to fishing!

This is our challenge, to not only believe and agree as to how we should live our lives - but to do it! How do we truly change, how do we know we have? I guess the only best answer is that we constantly work on that relationship with Jesus Christ every minute, every hour of every day. Maybe we involve others to hold us accountable.

It seems amazing to me how these key figures from the bible and of Jesus' Walk even struggled with 'going back to...' Just as amazing was how those living/existing with God in the Old Testament days even struggled to remain focused in their faith and GOD WAS THERE! Think about how challenging this is/will be for all of us. JESUS WAS ACTUALLY THERE and they still went back to fishing.

They 'saw' Him, knew Him, listened to Him, promised to Him and followed Him. But as soon as he 'poof' goes to where God and Jesus exist, Peter and others return to their old ways of living life.

How much harder is it now when we are to just 'believe' and through our faith lead a Walk like Jesus modeled and God taught us?

How are you doing...

It's your path to choose; others may walk it with you. No one can walk it for You.

These are the real questions for all of us:

- ✓ How strong is your faith?

- ✓ Are you totally IN about Jesus being real and you having a real relationship with Him?

- ✓ Where did you find Him and is your faith and belief really real?

- ✓ Is He your top relationship in life?

- ✓ Is your life really changed; are you changed; will you return to fishing and your old ways?

- ✓ Do you have other humans around you helping you; holding you accountable?

- ✓ Will you stay the course, stay on the right pathway, or ...continue trying different directions?

Peter answered him, "Though they all fall away because of you, I will never fall away." Matthew 26:33

SPACE FOR YOUR THOUGHT(S):

CONCLUDING COMMENTS

I believe our 'human' nature is to try to do it ourselves first, then look around for others to assist us and lastly in desperation, seek HIM. We believe we are in control...

We have surely got this all wrong, to include me. I am seeking Him 'first' way more than I used to; frequently I fail to do so. Interestingly enough it nearly always gets resolved in some sense when I do go to Him.

I hope this writing places renewed or brand new emphasis and focus on placing God & Jesus Christ in the proper place in your life. May "He's Number One" become the chant in your mind and heart as you move forward in your life? I can sure attest to the fact when I placed Him at the apex of that triangle, my life changed sincerely. I only wish I had found Him earlier, but then again, maybe that's GOD DOING THINGS IN HIS TIME. Lessons and learnings needed to happen first I am guessing. I needed to unpack that He is the only true COMPASS.

I will leave you with this challenge: take out the eternal insurance today; invite God and Jesus into your world. If He is there already, position Him in that top spot and watch life change.

SPACE FOR YOUR THOUGHT(S):

AUTHOR

President and Founder of Booker Training Associates; Doug is a Facilitator, Change Agent, Coach, Author & Leadership-Developer. Booker Training Associates is a business Doug began after a successful military career, retiring as a Major from the Army in 1992. The idea for his work evolved as Doug began realizing the 'challenge' facing organizations in managing (leading) people. Ultimately he focuses on organizational & individual leadership

behavior - helping not just the leader or manager, but with what he calls 'People-Systems'.

A strong believer in the need for continued learning, he has completed many certifications along with earning a Master's degree in Management. In his 20 years of serving organizations and individual leaders, Doug has worked with a variety of industries and also teaches in Higher Education with various universities. Along with his teaching and consulting work, he has now authored three books on Leadership and in 2012 completed 'SIGNIFICANCE Starts Now-How We Live Our Lives Matters' – a book focused on the individual and how we lead our lives.

Doug regards his wife Sydney, two children, siblings and extended family as the best parts of his life. A close 2nd is being able to work in a field that he loves and considers his passion, and maybe even a ministry of sorts.

Doug was selected as the Army's National Leadership Faculty of the Year in 1989; receiving this recognition from the Secretary of Defense in Washington D.C. Doug's favorite quote, which he asks people to hold him accountable to practice in life and work:

"People don't care how much you know, until they first know how much you care."

STATEMENT OF FAITH:

"I have been fortunate to work in a field that I love, helping people grow, for nearly 15 years now.

I have been very blessed, and because of this I want to give credit where it's due. I am a Christian and Believer. This is not a matter of preaching and forcing my beliefs on anyone; I would never approach this with your organization without your involvement and consent. I try to model what I believe in and let people make their own judgments.

My 'faith' is part of who I am, and a part of everything I do, say and believe. Jesus Christ is responsible for all I am and is 'totally' why I have successfully helped leaders, people, teams and overall organizations.

Principles and practices of real leadership are all totally aligned to the teachings of my faith. Relationships in my work - whether Executive Coaching or working with entire management teams. Clients nearly always become strong and lasting relationships, because of the base and foundation of my faith.

What does all this really mean to you as a client? Just that I will provide my services to you with trust, honesty, respect and helping you make leadership and working relationships better in your world."

www.bookertraining.com
913.232.0244

1521 Cole Rd, Sugar Creek, MO 64050

**Linked In & Facebook,
Twitter** (Booker Training) / etc

doug@bookertraining.com
(or)
bookertrainingassociates@gmail.com

"I would love to hear from you regarding this book or any of my other books as well. Always open for a talk about 'Leadership, Faith, People or God'. As well, I always enjoy adding new quality people to my life; so let's talk. God's best my friend."

Foreword &
Co-Authoring Contributions:

Christopher B Kirby MD

www.healingthehearts.com

BIO:

Born in Warrensburg, Missouri and graduated from Lexington High School. He received a BS with distinction in Biology and Doctor of Medicine (M.D.) from the University of Missouri, Kansas City School of Medicine. He completed an internship and residency in internal medicine at Wilford Hall Medical Center, San Antonio Texas.

He was board certified in Internal Medicine and completed recertification in Internal Medicine in 2012. He has served as Chief of Medicine and Chief of the Medical Staff at Parkland Medical Center, Derry, NH.

He is currently working and seeking additional fellowship training in the field of Addiction Medicine. He has worked and served in the ministries of Teen Challenge, New England and The Salvation Army and pursuing training in pastoral counseling.

He is very proud of his two children- Ryan and Brooke. He is active in both his church and the recovery community.

He currently resides in Tampa, Florida.

Previous books:

Leadership Conversations – Teaching Fishing, 2009

Leadership Conversations -   Rebuilding on Rock, 2010

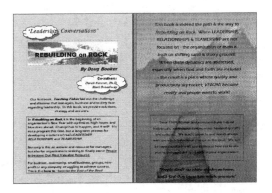

The Conference for Leaders, 2011

SIGNIFICANCE Starts Now – How We Live Our Lives Matters, 2012

My books can be found through my website or Amazon (to include Kindle); or you can always contact me directly for assistance. My next book will return to my work in Leadership, titled:
'KNOWINGLY LEADING – 25 Conversations to Success'

18678969R00057

Made in the USA
Middletown, DE
16 March 2015